Rembrandt

By Larry Silver

RIZZOLI ART SERIES

Series Editor: Norma Broude

Rembrandt

(1609–1669)

EVEN though he lived in seventeenth-century Holland, we think that we almost know Rembrandt. He has been the subject of popular, semifictional biographies and feature films, and we actually call him by his first name only. But current research has been drastically reshaping, even disassembling, our received notion of this artist and his work.[1]

In Amsterdam, a meticulous committee of academics and museum professionals, the Rembrandt Research Project, has been busy for three decades discriminating between a core of "authentic" Rembrandt paintings and a much larger group of "rejected" canvases, some of them among the most beloved and hallowed treasures of major museums.[2] Needless to say, not all "deattributions" have met with universal assent from scholars or from the general public. So even the starting point of this book, the paintings traditionally ascribed to Rembrandt, are subject to continuing scrutiny and debate.

At the same time, students of Rembrandt no longer celebrate him as the visionary loner and expressive genius of Romantic mythology evoked since the early nineteenth century. Instead, the critical reception of Rembrandt has been plumbed, reminding us that our seemingly natural viewing of his works has a changing history of its own.[3] Documents on the life—and the litigation—of the artist have revealed a seamier side to the actual ways of the painter than his sensitive works suggest, especially in terms of his relation to his closest relatives and the women in his life.[4] And scholars are still sorting out the complex web of relations between Rembrandt and his pupils, between Rembrandt and his patrons, and between Rembrandt and his artistic culture in seventeenth-century Holland.

Yet one reason for our sense of familiarity with this artist after more than three centuries is how much of himself he did share with us, chiefly through the depictions of his own face in drawings, etchings, and paintings that he made throughout his forty-four-year career—and seemingly right up to his final days.[5] Rembrandt used his own face for pictorial experiments, especially in his early drawings and etchings. In those works, he explored techniques of deep, evocative shadows as well as extremes of facial expression, such as grimaces or surprise, in order to convey emotion, whether brooding melancholy or theatrical interaction. Often Rembrandt would add costume embellishments— exotic turbans or the trappings of beggars, soldiers, or dandies—as if he were an actor trying out roles in his self-

representations. We need to remember while viewing such seemingly candid works that they actually represent calculated acts of self-definition, often employing poses tied to shifting wishes or adopted identities.[6] One painting (Dresden, c.1635) shows him together with his young bride, Saskia van Uylenburch, in the guise of the Prodigal Son.

Rembrandt's chosen role in life during the 1630s was that of the artist-as-gentleman. This role was defined for his generation by the model lives and self-portraits of the Flemish painters Peter Paul Rubens (1577–1640), artist and diplomat at the leading courts of Europe, and Anthony van Dyck (1599–1641), portraitist and courtier of the English king Charles I. The young Rembrandt codified his self-representation as the emulator of such elegant courtliness. His artistic models reached back to the previous century, to the very sources for both Rubens and Van Dyck: the Italian Renaissance masters Raphael and Titian. Living and working in the bustling port center of Amsterdam, Europe's economic center, Rembrandt was able to see renowned court portraits by Raphael (*Castiglione*) and Titian (the so-called *Ariosto*) come up for auction, and so he adapted their compositions into his own studied air of grace and nonchalance; leaning, for example, against a sill while dressed in a fashionable fur-trimmed jacket and beret (plate 2). Rembrandt's self-portraits of 1639–1640 make the bold claim that he had "arrived," both as a successful artist in a grand tradition (Raphael and Titian also used only their first names) and as a prominent, prosperous citizen of Amsterdam, peer to the fashionable patrons of his portraits.

The artist's rise had not been meteoric, but it had been steady. Son of a miller near the cloth center and university town of Leyden, Rembrandt Harmenszoon van Rijn had begun his training there, but he spent a formative period in 1624 in Amsterdam with Peter Lastman, painter of religious and mythic subjects, who (like Rubens and many other northern European artists) had lived for several years in Rome. His father was a member of the dominant religious group, the Calvinist Dutch Reformed Church, but his mother was a Roman Catholic, indicating in his own family the unusual degree of religious toleration then permitted in Holland. Despite the growing Dutch taste for landscapes or peasant scenes, Rembrandt's ambitions remained firmly fixed on the same "historical" themes used by Lastman.

In 1632 Rembrandt moved permanently to Amsterdam to try to make his fortune in the bustling port metropolis. Even while he continued to produce paintings of religious subjects as well as mythologies, his chief source of income in Amsterdam became portraits; recent scholarship reveals that he had a close network of patrons, which included many prominent Mennonites (a minority sect of orthodox Protestants) and prosperous merchants.[7] An art dealer, Hendrik van Uylenburch, with whom Rembrandt entered into a brief business partnership, introduced the artist to his cousin Saskia, and the couple married in 1634. Successes as a portraitist plus Saskia's dowry led Rembrandt in 1639 to purchase a large townhouse near Hendrik on the Breestraat, a newer district that had also become home to some of the wealthiest of the city's Portugese Jewish community (still bearing the name "Rembrandt's House," this site can be visited in modern Amsterdam). His successful and ambitious artistic career in cosmopolitan Amsterdam, reinforced by a stream of accomplished pupils

1. *Self-Portrait Drawing at a Window.* 1648.
Etching, 6¼ × 5⅛".
The British Museum, London

who also served as studio assistants, underlay that proud
and accomplished self-portrait that he began while
acquiring his new house (plate 2).

By the end of his career, however, when Rembrandt
produced another cluster of his most poignant self-portraits,
the entire character of his self-representation had changed
(fig. 1). Saskia had died after only a few years in the new
house, succumbing to complications during childbirth in
1642. Rembrandt's own debts connected with paying for his
house and for a substantial art collection finally caught up
with him in 1656, when he had to declare insolvency and
have his collection and other possessions inventoried for
liquidation. His years as gentleman-artist and collector had
ended.

Documents reveal a different Rembrandt, one who was
litigious, even mean-spirited. After Saskia's death he lived
together with a woman who later sued him for breach of
promise, and he then responded by having her remanded to
a house of correction. After 1649 he lived in common-law
marriage with Hendrickje Stoffels until her death in 1663.
Rembrandt's only child to survive past infancy was Titus,
who took over title to the Breestaat house and served with
Hendrickje as his father's "employer" in a legal maneuver
that enabled them to sell his artworks. In 1668, at the age of
twenty-six, Titus, too, predeceased Rembrandt, a scant year
before the artist's death and burial in the Reformed West
Church in Amsterdam.

When Rembrandt painted self-portraits during his final
decade, the 1660s, he unflinchingly showed himself with
the sagging flesh of old age but still with a firm, steady
gaze. In one image (plate 3), Rembrandt used his own
features for an image of Saint Paul, identified by his
traditional attributes of prayerbook and sword of martyrdom.
This picture forms one of a number of half-length images of
apostles and evangelists produced in 1661 (in another
canvas from the same series, Rembrandt used Titus as his
model for the angelic messenger accompanying Saint
Matthew). In contrast to the meticulous rendering and
subtle modeling of the earlier, extroverted self-portrait, this
late work employs bolder, visible brushwork and thoughtful
introspection. The choice of Saint Paul for this later
pictorial role confirms Rembrandt's own sense of humility
and personal piety after his travails; he was now more like

the penitent Prodigal Son than like the profligate he had
pictured earlier in the Dresden self-portrait with Saskia.

At the same time, this late self-portrait reveals
Rembrandt's ongoing interest in bringing out the human
dimensions of religious subjects through portraitlike
renderings. Throughout his career, Rembrandt would mark
his achievements by the fruitful mixture of those two
elements: portraits enlivened by dramatic movements and
gestures, complemented by fervent and literal religious
images of individuals made palpable by means of
portraitlike characterizations.

When, for example, Rembrandt took up the challenge of
painting the portrait of Uylenburch's minister, a draper who
was also the most esteemed Mennonite preacher in
Amsterdam, Cornelis Claesz. Anslo (1592–1646), he
attempted on a grand scale to convey the drama of the
orator by means of the visual rhetoric of setting and gesture
(plate 1). Rembrandt prepared his portrait with unusual
care, making two portrait drawings of Anslo from life, one of
which he then issued as an etching of the preacher (also in
1641). This image exemplifies the pastor's profession.
Within his book-lined study, the famous scholar has opened
his enormous Bible as he imparts a lesson to an attentive
listener, probably Anslo's wife, Aeltje Gerrtitsdr. Schouten;
thus his message is an intimate correction, based on
scripture and in accordance with the conduct of the
Mennonite creed. In essence, this emphasis on the spoken
word finding its proper audience is not only Rembrandt's
tribute to Anslo but also to the preacher's Protestant creed,
which stressed verbal sermons on God's holy word and
private meditation, in contrast to traditional Catholic
emphasis on altarpieces and religious art in the context of
the mass and public worship. In this image, the golden glow
of light falling on the open Bible despite the unlit candle
surely signifies spiritual revelation through the medium of
the Word.

Rembrandt also seems to have taken up an artistic
challenge in verses by a rival Dutchman, the poet Jost van
Vondel, to capture Anslo's magnetic speech in a soundless
image: "Ah Rembrandt, paint Cornelis's voice!/His visible
self is second choice/The invisible can only be known
through the word/To see Anslo truly, he must be heard."[8]

The year after completing his portrait of Anslo and his
wife, Rembrandt completed his largest group portrait, a
scene of the civic guard (the painting was once misnamed
the "Nightwatch" because of its seeming darkness, which
was caused by aged varnish that has now been removed by
careful restoration; plate 4). Amsterdam, like other Dutch
cities, maintained a cluster of such militia companies in
different quarters of the city as a form of civil defense, a
vestige of the Netherlands' war for independence from
Spain at the turn of the century. Similar group portraits of
militia companies (which were retained mostly as men's
clubs after the war) were painted in other cities, most
notably in the form of banquet scenes by Frans Hals in
nearby Haarlem between 1616 and 1639. Rembrandt's
group, a company of musketeers, was called the Kloveniers
(Dutch for "firearms"; other local Amsterdam militia
companies traditionally specialized in either longbows or
crossbows), and its Amsterdam district included such
drapers and merchants as Anslo and other Rembrandt
patrons. This large group portrait was commissioned in

2. *Portrait of Jan Six*. 1647. Etching, 10 × 7⅝". The British Museum, London

3. *The Three Trees*. 1643. Etching, 8½ × 11⅛". Museum of Fine Arts, Boston. Bequest of William Norton Bullard

about 1638 to decorate the new banqueting hall of the Kloveniers; the scheme included seven group portraits by various artists, among them a portrait of the Kloveniers board of governors.[9]

Front and center in the image, hand outstretched in a gesture reminiscent of Anslo's speaking, stands the company captain, Frans Banning Cocq, marked by a bright red sash and accompanied by his lieutenant, Willem van Ruijtenburch. The Kloveniers troop appears at full-length and accompanied by banners and drums, as if springing into action. The drama of the scene is further enhanced by means of Rembrandt's distinctive manipulations of areas of bright light and deep shadows, and the entire movement is composed through the enframing structure of a city gate as triumphal arch. The lively activity of the militia company relates to a specific, recent civic ceremony: the entry into the city of the queen mother of France in 1638, led by this very company. Both the martial air of musket preparation and the handsome costumes allude not only to a recent moment of glory for Cocq's company but also to the glory days of militias during the Dutch war for independence at the turn of the century. Rembrandt activated the group portrait through this concept of a collective force; departing from the usual lineup of individual portraits arrayed in a row or around a table, his energetic ensemble remains unique among similar militia company portrait commissions. At the end of his career, Rembrandt made another group portrait that depicts the sampling officials, or syndics, of the Amsterdam Drapers' Guild (plate 5), a commission that continued his lifelong support from the drapers profession.[10]

Rembrandt more frequently painted portraits of individuals. His likenesses range from the meticulous, spotlighted, descriptive renderings of features and surface textures in his formal early Amsterdam works of the 1630s to the broadly brushed character studies in soft tonal harmonies of his final two decades. Combining the virtues of both manners is the informal painting of *Jan Six* (plate 6). Rembrandt had known this art-loving patrician, a future burgomaster of Amsterdam, since 1645 and had sold him paintings as well as borrowed money from him.[11] In 1647 Rembrandt had made one of his most luminous portrait etchings of Six (fig. 2), a work of studied informality showing the handsome young man studying in a shadowy

interior (akin to the artist's own self-portrait etching of the following year; fig. 1) while surrounded by the trappings of his class: sword and mantle, artworks, and massive books (chiefly poetry; Six published plays and Latin poems). The painted portrait continues the tradition of courtly ease advanced by Rembrandt in his earlier self-portraits. Not only does the fashionable Six lightly wear his brilliant red mantle with gold buttons, but he dons his costly gloves carelessly; as if in echo of such detachment, the artist painted these accessories in broad, bold strokes, reserving his chief focus for the reflective visage of this distinctive sitter.

Rembrandt did not paint many landscapes, but he did devote considerable time to representing the Dutch countryside in his drawings and in a cluster of etchings that he made during the decade of the 1640s. In *The Three Trees* (fig. 3), he used dramatic shadows and heavy contrasts to enliven his native scenery with the appearance of an impending storm. The print is a virtuoso display of etching techniques with a full range of tones and of line-work, even while offering an anthology of Rembrandt's graphic representations of Dutch landscape. In similar fashion a few years later, Rembrandt's *The Mill* (plate 7) heroizes this most characteristic of Dutch constructions beneath the dramatic shadows of a gathering storm. Once again, tiny figures lend grandeur of scale to the mill, which is atop an imposing, distinctly un-Dutch bluff. This artificial rendering implies a fortresslike power for the very emblem of the Dutch nation, evoking both a patriotic pride as well as a tribute to Dutch cleverness in making productive use out of local forces of nature, as governed by God's munificence in accordance with contemporary Calvinist writings.

Many works of contemporary Dutch writing also attest to an admixture of such national pride with a pious consciousness of God's beneficence to the newly independent country.[12] Within the framework of the Dutch war for independence and for religious freedom, Dutch Calvinists often defined themselves in terms of the Old Testament tales of the "chosen people." This kind of nationalized version of the Bible prompted artists' interest in Old Testament subjects of providence or salvation, such as Rembrandt's dramatic use of the unusual theme of *Belshazzar's Feast* (plate 8). The source of this scene is the

4. *"Hundred Guilder Print" (Christ's Ministry).* c. 1649. Etching,
11¹⁄₈ × 16⁵⁄₁₆". The British Museum, London

5. Hendrick Terbrugghen. *Denial of Saint Peter.* 1624. Oil on
canvas, 52 × 70". © 1991 The Art Institute of Chicago. All rights
reserved. Charles H. and Mary F. S. Worcester Collection, 1969.3

Book of Daniel, in which the Babylonian's profanation of
vessels from the Temple of Jerusalem leads to his warning
by the moving finger that he and his empire would suffer a
downfall.

Frozen at the moment of maximum fear and horror,
Rembrandt's rendering contains all the drama of lighting,
costume, and gestures to be found in Rubens's or Lastman's
models. Rembrandt had prepared for the figure of the king
by making careful head studies (*tronies*) of turbaned figures,
especially of old men. His own drawn and etched self-
portraits preconditioned the open-mouthed expressions of
astonishment in *Belshazzar's Feast.* Precise Hebrew
lettering of the message of doom on the wall was derived
from the writings of Rabbi Menasseh ben Israel, a Portugese
Jew and neighbor of the artist on the Breestraat, whose
etched portrait Rembrandt produced in 1636. For this
large-scale and ambitious biblical subject, Rembrandt, like
the maker of a modern film epic, clearly felt the need for
historical accuracy and vivid evocation of events and
characters.

Yet a decade later Rembrandt's religious subjects display
the mood of quiet reflection that marked his self-portrait of
1648 (fig. 1). In one of his most ambitious prints, *Christ's
Ministry* (fig. 4), he arrayed an image of Christ preaching to
a multitude as if it were a stilled *"Nightwatch"* group
portrait. The overall message, drawn from Matthew 19, is a
sermon that the poor and the afflicted, not the rich and
powerful, will receive divine grace. For the portraitlike head
of Christ, Rembrandt had made numerous painted studies,
possibly using a Jewish model in his neighborhood, and
both the costumes and the faces of the crowd in this print
may also derive from the local Jewish community. The
painted equivalent of *Christ's Ministry* is the *Supper at
Emmaus* (plate 9), in which a soft and atmospheric glow
emanates from Christ in place of the glaring and brilliant
light of the divine in *Belshazzar's Feast* (plate 8). Quiet
contemplation replaces gestural action.

The portraitlike studies of individual heads for biblical
subjects led Rembrandt eventually to focus his attention on
the human dimension of sacred narrative, particularly the
emotional and thought-filled reactions of the principals.
Without including David in the image at all, Rembrandt
evokes in *Bathsheba* (plate 10) the uncertain moment when
the protagonist, a married woman, receives a solicitous
letter from the king. In all likelihood Hendrickje sat as

model for this beautiful, full-bodied nude, and there might
well be a biographical overtone to this subject, since in the
same year Hendrickje was admonished by Reformed
Church authorities because she and Rembrandt were
openly living together (she also bore him a daughter three
months later). Rembrandt represented the female nude
occasionally in his graphic works, but in his paintings such
figures are quite rare. Whether or not one wishes to infer
Rembrandt's own tender feelings toward his companion
Hendrickje in this work, he certainly implicates the viewer,
taking the place of King David, who spied on Bathsheba as
she bathed, in the voyeuristic contemplation of her beauty.
At the same time, the artist reminds the viewer that this
attractive woman, contrasted in her youthful nudity with the
clothed and aged servant who washes her feet, has her own
complex thoughts, particularly about a proposal to adultery,
so that she cannot simply be regarded in her isolation as an
object of male desire.

Internal struggle and thoughtfulness also register on the
face of an apostle in Rembrandt's staging in the *Denial of
Saint Peter* (plate 11), a climax of Rembrandt's mysterious
nocturnes. The use of a hidden candle as the sole light
source for a night scene had already been pioneered during
the 1620s by Utrecht artists, particularly Hendrick
Terbrugghen (fig. 5) and Gerrit Honthorst, who had recently
returned from Rome and painted their own versions of the
same subject. Though we do not know specifics about
Rembrandt's audience for such works, Terbrugghen's picture,
painted by a Catholic artist for a Catholic audience, reveals
the degree to which Rembrandt, like Rubens and these
Utrecht painters, still clung to a heritage of religious art.

The pensive face of Saint Peter also resembles the
furrowed brows and shadowed eyes of Rembrandt's late self-
portrait as Saint Paul from the following year (plate 3) and
signals a kinship with the series of half-length apostles and
evangelists he painted in about 1660. Here, more than ever,
Rembrandt's ability to capture the human dimension of a
biblical scene emerges from his experience as a portraitist
as well as from his constant ability to manipulate mood
through light and shadow. He would employ the same
talents in his mythic themes and histories.

Rembrandt's approach to mythological subjects conforms
closely to his treatment of religious events. For example, in
all likelihood Rembrandt posed his new bride Saskia in the
guise of the goddess of flowers and of spring for his *Portrait*

of Saskia Dressed as Flora (plate 13). The same rich description of costume seen in *Belshazzar's Feast* is employed in the service of sumptuous brocades and flowering garlands. In glorifying, even mythologizing his own bride, Rembrandt was emulating the artistry of Rubens, who had remarried shortly before and then fused the features of his young wife with the faces of Venus and other goddesses. Pygmalions in reverse, both artists seem to want to make art out of life. In Rembrandt's Holland, however, the taste for pastoral subjects and the association of high-born ladies with shepherdess costumes were current aristocratic art fashion. Indeed, in 1636 Rembrandt's pupil Govert Flinck painted a double portrait of the artist and Saskia dressed as a shepherd couple. Throughout the 1630s, as Rembrandt's own self-portraits frequently indulged his delight in role-playing and wearing exotic or sumptuous costumes, his images of Saskia partook of the same fantasy. Rembrandt's depiction of his wife in this painting should be seen as the embodiment of the pastoral ideal, the latest courtly mode, fused onto a grand mythological model, possibly derived from a Titian prototype (then in an Amsterdam collection) of the goddess of fertility.

Despite employing mythological subjects, Rembrandt never traveled to Italy, as Rubens and the Utrecht painters had, but his fame even in his lifetime was such that his works were in demand there as well. In 1652 Don Antonio Ruffo, a Sicilian collector in Messina, negotiated for a Rembrandt painting and left the subject up to the artist.[13] The resulting work was *Aristotle with a Bust of Homer* (plate 14). Although principally another half-length, portraitlike study of the ancient sage, this image shows Aristotle in his dual role as author of the *Poetics* and student of literary classics (the bust of Homer) and as the teacher for a great princely patron, Alexander the Great. The implied presence of Alexander is signaled by the lustrous, almost palpable chain of office, upon which hangs a pendant medallion with a profile portrait of Aristotle's princely patron. Dressed in the sumptuous imaginary costume of a courtier and touching his chain with his idle left hand, Aristotle nonetheless turns his introspective gaze as well as the focused touch of his right hand to the bust of the great poet, as if to signal that a tension exists between his two roles. Rembrandt might even be suggesting here, through the wistful inclination of the sage's head, that the poetic creativity of Homer, akin to the artistry of the painter himself, remains superior to the active accomplishment of Alexander or even to the contemplative philosophy and alternative moral instruction of Aristotle himself. The association of a living figure with the classical bust of his professional hero derives from a portrait formula perfected by Rubens in the 1620s.

One of Rembrandt's final visualizations of myth concerned the legendary founding of independent Holland in the days of ancient Rome.[14] For the main gallery of the sumptuous new Town Hall on the Dam Square of Amsterdam, Rembrandt was commissioned to replace a work by his former pupil Flinck (who died in 1660). The assignment was to paint the *Oath of Claudius Civilis* (plate 12). In essence, the solemn scene he painted can be taken almost as an inversion of *Belshazzar's Feast*, a tale of liberation told from the point of view of the bold revolutionaries. The primitive Dutchmen, or Batavians, as they were known to Tacitus and the Romans, gathered in confederation under the sky in a forest by night; they then went on to achieve a resounding defeat of the Roman legions on the Rhine and to gain political autonomy, presaging the Dutch revolt against Spain in the sixteenth century. At the same time the political oath of confederation anticipated the current, federal system of government in Holland.

Rembrandt's painting, now greatly cut down and removed from its original Town Hall context, stages the oath as a sacred rite, aglow with the charge of shared risk (conveyed by the device of the hidden candle, as in the contemporary *Denial of Saint Peter*). A chalice before the crowned head of Civilis himself suggests spiritual communion, while the joining of swords seals the tribal pact. The martial leader displays his blinded eye, an awe-inspiring scar from previous heroic combat. Indeed, the very contentiousness of Rembrandt's vision might well have sealed the unhappy fate of his canvas, assuring that the peace-loving merchants of Amsterdam's government would find the image offensive to their politics of trade and prosperity. Yet even in its present state, cut down and reworked by Rembrandt, the *Oath of Claudius Civilis* recaptures some of the dignity of religious works, such as the *Supper at Emmaus*, in a group covenant intensified with nationalism. At the same time it conveys the portraitlike vigor and compositional unity of Rembrandt's last works, such as the *Syndics* (plate 5).

No single painting can encapsulate the accomplishment of so varied a painter as Rembrandt, but one late work seems to bestride his major interests while remaining an evocative mystery. The moving interaction of a loving couple in the painting now nicknamed "The Jewish Bride" (plate 15) has been taken to be a double portrait in biblical guise, akin to Rembrandt's dressing-up for his own self-portraits or his rendering of Saskia as Flora. Biographically-minded scholars have tried to see the faces of Titus and Magdalena van Loo, his new bride of 1668, in this work (and have dated it accordingly), yet the individual identity of this pair has never been firmly established and their features appear more generalized than most commissioned likenesses by Rembrandt. Moreover, the richly colored and lavishly brushed costumes of the couple suggest that they, too, should be viewed as having been displaced into ancient times and exotic locales.

But where and when? Specific biblical suggestions, such as Isaac and Rebecca or Jacob and Rachel, have not received clear assent from scholars, because the scenic accessories of the Old Testament stories are lacking here, though biblical ancestors seem more probable than any proposed scenes drawn from ancient history.[15] Only the loving relationship of this couple is assured, and their marriage seems likely, as he bestows a chain around her and she in turn holds a fruit, the traditional emblem of marital fertility. Some scholars have suggested that Rembrandt used such subjects with minimal narrative detail precisely in order to generalize about universal aspects of the human condition—in this case, thought-filled yet loving intimacy.

With this picture, we see a prototype of Rembrandt's evocative strengths: what could be intended as a biblical (or ancient) subject comes to life as surely as if it were a costumed portrait based on live models. In the quiet hush inherent in the medium of painting, Rembrandt shows believable individuals lost in their own private thoughts and attempting to bridge an ineffable isolation while seemingly unconscious of being objects of a viewer's gaze. But the kinds of identifying features and historical information so necessary for understanding other Rembrandt pictures are absent here. We know neither the intended religious subject nor the identity of the sitters—if any—for these narrative roles. We do not know any circumstances of its creation or its first owners. In the midst of all the revisions and investigative demythification of the artist-hero favored by prior generations, Rembrandt's imagery still has the capacity to retain a sense of depth—and mystery.

NOTES

1. Julius Held, *Rembrandt Studies* (Princeton: Princeton University Press, 1991), pp. 3–16.
2. *A Corpus of Rembrandt Paintings* (The Hague: Nijhoff, 1982–present), 3 volumes published to date (1992).
3. Seymour Slive, *Rembrandt and His Critics 1630–1730* (The Hague: Nijhoff, 1953); Jan Emmens, *Rembrandt en de regels van de Kunst* (Utrecht: Haentjens, Dekker, and Gumbert, 1968), with English summary; Held, *Rembrandt Studies*, pp. 144–152.
4. Walter Strauss and Marjon van der Meulen, *The Rembrandt Documents* (New York: Abaris, 1979); Gary Schwartz, *Rembrandt: His Life, His Paintings* (New York: Viking, 1985).
5. Perry Chapman, *Rembrandt's Self-Portraits* (Princeton: Princeton University Press, 1989).
6. Chapman, *Rembrandt's Self-Portraits*; Svetlana Alpers, *Rembrandt's Enterprise* (Chicago: University of Chicago Press, 1989), pp. 34–87.
7. Gary Schwartz, *Rembrandt: His Life, His Paintings*, pp. 132–142.
8. Jan Emmens, "Ay Rembrandt, maal Cornelis stem," *Nederlands Kunsthistorisch Jaarboek* 7 (1956), pp. 133–166; the translation from Vondel's Dutch verses is that of Schwartz, *Rembrandt*, pp. 217–219.
9. Egbert Haverkamp-Begemann, *Rembrandt: "The Nightwatch"* (Princeton: Princeton University Press, 1982).
10. H. van de Waal, "The Syndics and Their Legend," *Steps Towards Rembrandt* (Amsterdam: North-Holland, 1974), pp. 247–292.
11. David Smith, "'I Janus': Privacy and the Gentlemanly Ideal in Rembrandt's Portraits of Jan Six," *Art History* 11 (1988), pp. 42–63.
12. Simon Schama, *The Embarrassment of Riches* (New York: Knopf, 1987), pp. 93–125.
13. Held, *Rembrandt Studies*, pp. 17–58.
14. Margaret Deutsch Carroll, "Civic Ideology and Its Subversion: Rembrandt's *Oath of Claudius Civilis*," *Art History* 9 (1986), pp. 12–35; van de Waal, *Steps Towards Rembrandt*, pp. 28–43.
15. Christian Tümpel, *Rembrandt. Mythos und Methode* (Königstein: Langewiesche, 1986), pp. 119–123; also pp. 141–146 on Rembrandt and Amsterdam Jews. Tümpel cites precedents in prints for similar depictions of the theme of Isaac and Rebecca observed by Abimelech. Tümpel also argues against the likelihood that any "disguised" portraits of living sitters appear in this painting; that mistaken idea derives in his opinion from the complete extrication of the subject from its usual narrative fullness (and he cites the example of *Aristotle*; Alpers, *Rembrandt's Enterprise*, pp. 86–87, reaches similar conclusions).

FURTHER READING

Bomford, David, et al. *Art in the Making. Rembrandt.* London: The National Gallery, 1988.

Brown, Christopher, et al. *Rembrandt. The Master and His Workshop.* New Haven: Yale University Press, 1991.

Gerson, Horst. *Rembrandt Paintings.* New York: Reynal, 1968.

Gods, Saints and Heroes. Dutch Painting in the Age of Rembrandt. Washington, D.C.: National Gallery of Art, 1980.

Haak, Bob. *Rembrandt: His Life, His Work, His Time.* New York: Abrams, 1969.

———. *The Golden Age.* New York: Abrams, 1984.

Rosenberg, Jakob. *Rembrandt: Life and Work,* 2nd ed. London: Phaidon, 1964; reprint Ithaca: Cornell University Press, 1980.

Rosenberg, Jakob, Seymour Slive, and E. H. ter Kuile. *Dutch Art and Architecture*, 3rd ed. Harmondsworth: Penguin, 1984.

Schneider, Cynthia. *Rembrandt's Landscapes.* New Haven: Yale University Press, 1990.

Silver, Larry, "Rembrandt." *Encyclopaedia Britannica*, vol. 26 (1988 ed.).

Sumowski, Werner. *Gemälde der Rembrandt-Schüler.* Landau: PVA, 1983–present, 4 vols.

White, Christopher. *Rembrandt.* London: Thames and Hudson, 1984.

In loving memory of my father, Jack Silver, my mother, Doris Sprecher Silver, and her mother, Sarah Goldberg Sprecher, who taught me to rejoice in beautiful books, particularly books about artworks.

First published in 1992 in the United States of America by Rizzoli International Publications, Inc.
300 Park Avenue South
New York, New York 10010

Library of Congress Cataloging-in-Publication Data
Silver, Larry, 1947–
   Rembrandt / Larry Silver
     p.   cm. — (Rizzoli art series)
   Includes bibliographical references.
   ISBN 0-8478-1519-6
   1. Rembrandt, Harmenszoon van Rijn, 1606–1669.
   2. Artists—Netherlands—Biography.   I. Title.   II. Series.
N6953.R4S524   1992
760'.092—dc20   91-33472
                                CIP

Series Editor: Norma Broude

Series designed by José Conde and Nicole Leong/Rizzoli

Printed in Singapore

Index to Colorplates

1. *Portrait of Cornelis Claesz. Anslo and His Wife.* 1641. This double portrait of a renowned Mennonite preacher and his wife uses gesture to suggest the rhetorical power of the orator and uses the illuminated book to convey the importance of the Protestant Word.

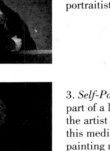

2. *Self-Portrait Leaning on a Sill.* 1640. Rembrandt's most confident self-portrait, painted at the height of his prosperity as a portraitist in Amsterdam, emulates the models of the great Italian Renaissance portraitists Raphael and Titian.

3. *Self-Portrait as Apostle Paul.* 1661. As part of a late series of saints and apostles, the artist here adapts his own features in this meditative reflection on aging. The painting might be seen as a personalized Protestant creed about inner spirituality.

4. *"Nightwatch" (Militia Company of the Kloveniers).* 1642. The largest of Rembrandt's group portraits renders a militia company of musketeers while evoking the glory days such volunteer companies enjoyed during the Dutch war of independence half a century earlier.

5. *Syndics of the Clothmakers' Guild.* 1662. Rembrandt's last important public group portrait depicts the samplers of the cloth guild, an important Dutch industrial group and a consistent patron of Rembrandt's individual and group portraits.

6. *Jan Six.* 1654. A future burgomaster of Amsterdam as well as a poet, playwright, and art collector, who also ended up as one of the artist's demanding creditors, is the subject of one of Rembrandt's most informal painted portraits.

7. *The Mill.* c.1645. Despite controversy concerning its attribution to Rembrandt, especially after recent cleaning, this painting nonetheless exemplifies Rembrandt's distinctively dramatized representation of Dutch scenery, while including a monumentalized typical local structure more commonly seen in his etched landscapes.

8. *Belshazzar's Feast.* c.1636–1638. In one of his most monumental and theatrical paintings, Rembrandt portrays an Old Testament subject (Daniel 5) with dramatic gestures and costumes to comment on the relationship between sacrilege and political consequences, a favorite Dutch concern during this era of religious conflicts.

9. *Supper at Emmaus.* 1648. Rembrandt achieves a quiet realization of Christ's humble yet spiritual presence as well as the private moments of recognition by his apostles; like most of Rembrandt's religious figures, Christ's portrait is based on individual head studies made by the artist, probably after a Jewish model from his neighborhood.

10. *Bathsheba.* 1654. Using as his model his common-law wife, Hendrickje Stoffels, Rembrandt realizes the interior thoughts of a beautiful Old Testament adulteress.

11. *Denial of Saint Peter.* 1660. Rembrandt here reprises a favorite theme and frequent pictorial device, a nocturne broken by a brilliant hidden candle; this theme and motif had already employed by Utrecht artists during the 1620s in order to convey the moral dilemma of the apostle at his moment of crisis in betraying Christ.

12. *Oath of Claudius Civilis.* 1661. Although a major commission for the new Amsterdam Town Hall (largely decorated by Rembrandt's own pupils), this painting was rejected by city officials and later cut down by the artist. It recounts the plot of the ancient Dutch tribe, the Batavians, against the foreign domination of Rome, and it was conceived as an allegory of the war for independence from Catholic Spain.

13. *Portrait of Saskia Dressed as Flora.* 1634. Celebrating the goddess of spring and of fertility, this mythological figure incorporates the form of Rembrandt's new bride, Saskia van Uylenburch, and demonstrates the artist's love of costume and rich color; in the process, Rembrandt emulates the prior example of Rubens as well as current Dutch court fashion for pastoral subjects.

14. *Aristotle.* 1653. Commissioned for a Sicilian art patron, this classical subject evokes the conflict between artistic creativity (symbolized by the bust of Homer) and court responsibility (Aristotle's chain of office) within the vocations of the ancient philosopher of both politics and poetics.

15. *"The Jewish Bride."* c.1666. Though possibly presenting a double portrait of a couple in the guise of Old Testament exemplars, probably Isaac and Rebecca, this late work reveals minimal specifics of its narrative subject in order to emphasize the universality of tender love between private individuals.

1. *Portrait of Cornelis Claesz. Anslo and His Wife.* 1641. Oil on canvas, 69 1/4 x 83 7/16".
Gemäldegalerie, Staatliche Museen Preussischer Kulturbesitz, Berlin

2. *Self-Portrait Leaning on a Sill*. 1640. Oil on canvas, 40 ⅛ x 31½".
The National Gallery, London

3. *Self-Portrait as Apostle Paul*. 1661. Oil on canvas, 36⅛ x 30⅜".
Rijksmuseum-Foundation, Amsterdam

4. *"Nightwatch"* (*Militia Company of Kloveniers*). 1642. Oil on canvas, 143³⁄₁₆ x 172¼".
Rijksmuseum-Foundation, Amsterdam

11. *Denial of Saint Peter.* 1660. Oil on canvas, 61 ⅛ x 67 ³/₁₆".
Rijksmuseum-Foundation, Amsterdam

12. *Oath of Claudius Civilis*. 1661. Oil on canvas, 77 ⅛ x 122 ⁵⁄₁₆".
The National Art Museums of Sweden, Stockholm. Photograph: Statens Konstmuseer

13. *Portrait of Saskia Dressed as Flora*. 1634. Oil on canvas, 49 x 40".
Hermitage Museum, St. Petersburg. Photograph by Art Resource

14. *Aristotle with a Bust of Homer*. 1653. Oil on canvas, 56 ½ x 53 ¾".
The Metropolitan Museum of Art, New York. Purchased with special funds and gifts of friends of the Museum, 1961

15. *"The Jewish Bride."* c.1666. Oil on canvas. 48 3/16 x 66 5/16".
Rijksmuseum-Foundation, Amsterdam